HERB
TOPIARIES

SALLY GALLO

INTERWEAVE PRESS

HERB TOPIARIES

by Sally Gallo

Illustrations by Sally Gallo

Design and cover illustration by Susan Strawn

Production by Linda Kirchgesler/Colorado Typographics

Copyright 1992 by Sally Gallo

All rights reserved

Library of Congress Cataloging-in-Publication Data:
Gallo, Sally, 1939–
    Herb topiaries / Sally Gallo.
      p.   cm.
    Includes bibliographical references.
    ISBN 0-934026-79-3 : $6.95
    1. Topiary work. 2. Herbs—Training. 3. Herbs—
Pruning. 4. Herb gardening. 5. Container
gardening. I. Title.
SB463.G34   1992
635'.7—dc20   92-38638
                                    CIP

First printing: 5M: 1092:CT/OB

INTERWEAVE PRESS
201 East Fourth Street
Loveland, Colorado 80537

To the memory of my chief assistant—my husband

 Acknowledgments

I am grateful to the staff
and library at Bittersweet
Hill Nurseries in
Davidsonville, Maryland,
and to Elaine Lahn, who
expanded it with her
creative new designs for
scented geranium
standards and enhanced it
with skilled care.

Contents

Introduction

WITH INCREASED INTEREST in herb cultivation during recent years, more gardeners are discovering the decorative possibilities of plants that have been carefully trained and trimmed into ornamental shapes. Container-grown herb topiaries can graciously frame an entryway or decorate a table or windowsill, and generally enhance decor, whether indoors or out. The time and effort spent in maintaining one of these green sculptures are repaid in the charm and beauty it brings to a room or garden, and sometimes also in the culinary dividend of its trimmings.

Raising topiaries in containers indoors began to interest American gardeners during the 1950s, with the resurgence in popularity of house plants after a lapse of about half a century, but the first recorded use of trained plants dates back to the first century B.C. and the Romans. It was they who gave us the term "topiary", from the Latin *topia*, an ornamental garden, which was supervised by a garden designer or *topiarius*.

In the centuries that followed, the art of topiary developed further in Renaissance Italy, France, and England, appearing about 1690 in America at Williamsburg, Virginia, where plants were trained in geometric shapes to accent knot gardens. The tradition continues today in certain public and private gardens both in collections of shrubs that have been shaped into elaborate menageries of animal forms and in herbal knot gardens accented with the simpler standards—specimens trained with an erect center stem and a carefully shaped spherical or conical top.

TOPIARY
BASICS

Starting an Herb Standard

MOST TOPIARIES are produced from upright-growing woody herbs such as those described later in Plants for Topiaries, beginning on page 31. They begin their career as cuttings, except for the occasional mature plant discovered to have a central straight stem.

Because successfully rooting woody herbs requires a certain amount of skill, the easiest way for a novice gardener to obtain suitable cuttings is to purchase them, already rooted, from a reliable nursery. Look for a plant with a single, very straight stem and no side growth. I'd suggest you start with one in a 3-inch (7.5 cm) pot. If you are ordering by mail, mention that you want to make the plant into a topiary.

To start your own cuttings, use a container at least 2 inches (5 cm) deep in which drainage holes can easily be punched. An aluminum foil baking pan is fine. If the container has held soil before, wash it, then sterilize it with a solution of one part chlorine bleach to five parts water. Nearly fill the container with a mixture of half perlite and half vermiculite that is just damp. (The dry mixture is light and fluffy; when damp, it will be darker in color and will hold together more readily.)

The plants from which you plan to take cuttings should have been recently watered. Dip the blade of a sharp knife or razor blade or the tip of curved pruners in alcohol to sterilize it and take a slip of new tender growth 2 inches (5 cm) or longer, slicing diagonally just below a leaf node. Remove the lower leaves of the cutting, make a hole in the rooting medium no more than 1/4 inch (0.6 cm) across with a pencil or stick, and insert the cutting. Because oxygen is as important as moisture to the cutting's health, don't pack the medium at all. It may be beneficial to dip older, woodier cuttings in a rooting hormone such as Rootone, preferably with fungicide, before sticking them in the rooting medium. It is not necessary to treat new, soft growth with the hormone; in fact, it is likely to burn the tender stems.

I have started scented geraniums in blocks of Oasis floral foam, though the perlite/vermiculite mixture described above is also successful. Simply plant the Oasis block directly into a pot when it has grown full of roots.

Whichever medium you choose, space cuttings so that they don't touch; adequate air circulation is one of the keys to successful rooting.

The best season for taking most cuttings is spring, when plants are producing new growth. Sweet bay and lemon verbena cuttings are best rooted in late July to early August, however, and those of rosemary may be taken in late summer and fall as well as in the spring. Though they may root eventually, all plants seem to take longer in winter.

After placing all cuttings in the rooting medium, move them to a bright, sunny spot such as a windowsill and cover them with a sheet of tissue paper for a few days to a week. This shields them from the sun and maintains humidity while allowing good air circulation. Cuttings covered tightly are prone to rotting. In the winter, I set the trays of cuttings on a heated table, which cuts rooting time from four to six weeks to as little as three weeks. Fairly inexpensive, thermostatically controlled heating cables for this purpose are available from garden supply catalogs. Mist the cuttings as necessary to keep them from wilting; they dry out very quickly when on a heating cable. After removing the tissue paper, you may need to mist more frequently and/or shade the cuttings until they have become acclimated to their new conditions.

To ascertain whether a cutting has rooted, hold it between thumb and forefinger and gently tug upward. When rooted sufficiently, the tiny plant won't move, whereas an unrooted cutting will lift right out of the perlite/vermiculite mix.

Training Topiary Standards

Early Training

TRAINING BEGINS EARLY for rooted cuttings that are destined to become topiaries. The first step is to transplant the young 3- to 4-inch-tall (7–10 cm) plants from the rooting medium into 3-inch (7.5 cm) pots. Choose a potting mixture that drains quickly, such as Pro-Mix, a soilless mix, or equal amounts of aged compost, sand, and peat. (To test drainage, fill a pot three-quarters full of potting mix and flood with water; it should pour out the drainage hole. If water stands, the mix is too heavy.) After potting, insert a short, slender, 10- or 12-inch (25–30 cm) bamboo stake, such as a barbecue skewer, about half an inch to an inch (1–2.5 cm) away from the plant. Tie the plant loosely to the stake with one or two loops of cotton string. As the plant grows, add successive loops near the top to keep it growing upright. Some growers use a plastic drinking straw, split down its side and positioned around the delicate stem of the cutting, in this early stage of training.

A few months later, when the plant has reached the height of the stake and begins to outgrow its small pot, transplant it again, this time to a 5- or 6-inch (12–15 cm) pot. At this time, replace the original stake with a new bamboo garden stake which is as long as the intended height of the mature tree. Push the stake deep into the pot an inch (2.5 cm) from the plant's stem and tie the plant loosely to it at frequent intervals with strips of cloth or raffia (string is not wide enough).

The Shape of Things to Come   Now is the time to determine the ultimate form of the topiary. Observe the plant's pattern of growth. Are twigs bunching at one or more points along the stem as well as at the top? It may hold promise of a double- or triple-tier shape. On the other hand, it may suggest a less geometric form such as a fanciful animal or bird.

SINGLE BALL The secret of effective topiary design is simplicity of form and correct pruning. The simplest design is the standard, (also known as the poodle or lollipop), consisting of a single head of foliage clipped into a tight ball. Any of the plants discussed in this book may be trained in this shape, though some are more appealing when allowed to grow into a less formal, naturally open head of arching branches. Either shape is achieved by pinching the topmost growth, or leader, when the plant has grown to the desired height.

Single Ball

Begin trimming the lowest leaves and branches from the stem at the time of the plant's transfer to its 5- or 6-inch (12–15 cm) pot. The green head should measure one-third the total length of the stem—1 foot (30 cm) for a 3-foot (1 m) topiary—for a pleasing, balanced appearance and adequate photosynthesis to keep the plant growing well.

After you've clipped the leader and the tips of the side branches, just relax and watch the foliage start to fill in and the head begin to take shape. This process usually takes a few months, depending on which herb you are working with. When the shape has been achieved, maintain it by clipping the new growth as it appears, about every other week during periods of rapid growth in the spring and summer, seldom or not at all in winter. As the plants become large, you may transplant them to 7- or 8-inch (17–20 cm) clay pots.

Multiple Balls

Mature plants that have become pot-bound need an annual, sometimes twice-annual, root pruning to keep them in the same pot. See page 28 for directions.

MULTIPLE BALLS Another popular shape consists of one or more additional balls of foliage on the stem. It's achieved by training branches that are growing close together naturally along the stem and cutting off all growth in between. Trim all the balls to the same size unless you would like tiers that become progressively smaller from bottom to top.

CONE Another variation of the single head is a cone that is large at the bottom, beginning at the

Cone

rim of the pot for a Christmas tree effect—particularly appropriate for an upright rosemary—or commencing farther up the stem. A cone can also top a multiple-tier topiary. These more complex designs require small-leaved, tightly compact plants such as Greek myrtle, rosemary, and Victorian rosemary.

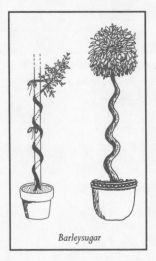

Barleysugar

BARLEYSUGAR A bit more complex is the form traditionally called barleysugar, in which the shaped head surmounts a trunk which has been wound into a corkscrew. This style of trunk looks best topped with a plain globe of green, for here the focus is on the stem. Select a six-month-old plant and transplant it to a 5- or 6-inch (12–15 cm) pot. Insert a stout stake— I use 3/4-inch (2 cm) bamboo—into the pot and trim it to two-thirds the height of the plant, leaving the top growth free. Now, carefully wind the still-flexible stem evenly around the stake. Tie the stem snugly to the stake, but check the ties in two or three weeks and loosen them as soon as they start to become tight. Trim the leader and side branches as described for the single-head design (page 14). As the tree grows taller, continue removing the lowest branches and winding and tying the stem around the stake, checking previous ties for tightness.

When the plant has reached the height of the stake and the stem has stiffened somewhat (this can take anywhere from six months to a year, depending on height), remove all the ties and, starting at the top, very gently unwind the stem from around the stake. Pulling the stake out or unwinding too woody a specimen will injure the stem. After unwinding the stem, support the topiary with another stake the same thickness as the trunk. The spirals should look evenly spaced. As the trunk thickens with age, the spirals become less prominent and more subtly wavy. Nothing can equal a matched pair of these elegant topiaries stationed at a formal entranceway, on a patio, or in a sunroom.

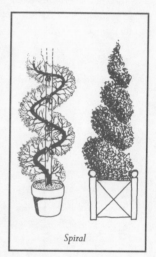

Spiral

I have made barleysugar topiaries with 3-foot-tall (1 m) Greek myrtles and plan to experiment with 'Lemon Crispum' scented geraniums. Young, flexible Victorian rosemaries could conceivably be trained in this manner, too, but their stems tend to be more brittle than those of other species.

SPIRAL A variation on the barleysugar style turns the entire tree into a layered green spiral from the rim of the pot to the top. Instead of wrapping the stem closely around the stake, form it into wider loops that extend away from the stake as you wind, and tie them where they intersect with the stake (see illustration). Usually, the loop at the bottom is largest, with successive ones becoming progressively smaller toward the top. Evenly space the loops rather far apart vertically, too, so the foliage of each turn will not grow into the one above it and obscure the shape. Do not remove any growth nor pinch the leader until the tree is as tall as you want it. This shape needs to be kept closely trimmed to be effective. I use Greek myrtle for the spiral form, though I see no reason why rosemary, small-leaved scented geraniums, or gray santolina could not also be trained this way.

Topiary Gems in Rings and Crowns

Topiary plants may be trained on any of several styles of wire rings: a single circle, a heart shape, or two rings wired together with a smaller one attached to the top to create a "crown ring". I've used 'Lockwood de Forest' and 'Huntington Carpet' prostrate rosemaries as well as 'Prince Rupert', 'French Lace', 'Lemon Crispum', and 'Strawberry' small-leaved scented geraniums.

Single Ring

SINGLE RING OR HEART To form a single wire ring for a 4-inch (10 cm) clay pot or other container (see Choosing the Right Container, page 21), bend a 23-inch (58 cm) length of aluminum wire the thickness of a coat hanger around a 6-inch (15 cm) cylinder (such as the top of a clay pot), twisting together the excess wire at the ends. Stop twisting about 1 1/2 inches (4 cm) from the ends and with pliers, bend them out sideways as shown. Suspend the ring on a rod such as an old broom handle and spray paint it a light sage green that will blend with the plant stems. When the paint is dry, stand the twisted stem of the ring in the pot. (For a larger pot, make the ring at least as wide as the width of the pot.) Partly fill the pot with fast-draining potting medium (see pages 13 & 25) and tamp it down to keep the ring upright. A heart shape is formed by simply bending a single ring downward at the top before placing it in the pot.

Select a rosemary or geranium plant having at least one long branch—preferably two or more—and place it in the pot right next to the ring. This could be a recently rooted cutting, but even a mature plant in a 6-inch (15 cm) pot can be shaped in this way.

For a plant with just one branch, start at the bottom of the ring winding the branch around and up one side; secure it loosely with green cotton string. It will eventually grow all the way around the circle. Emerging side shoots may be pinched to make the ring of foliage bushier, or a side shoot near the base may be left to grow and tied onto the other side of the ring.

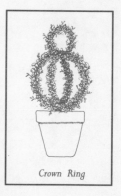

Crown Ring

For a multibranched plant, train the branches up either side of the ring and pinch the side shoots to encourage bushiness.

When the plant has grown sufficiently to extend all around the ring (a matter of four to six months for a rooted cutting, less for a more mature plant), clip the branch tips to force further branching and thicken the shape. To discourage fungus diseases, keep your ring in full sun with good ventilation, and when watering, avoid splashing the leaves. Continue close trimming as the plant grows.

CROWN RING A crown ring employs two single circles of wire joined at right angles, then tightly wrapped with florist's wire at the top where they cross. At the bottom, the twisted ring ends are wired together to form a single strong shaft. A smaller top ring formed with thinner wire is attached as shown. If the latter leans or wobbles, it can be reinforced with more florist's wire. Place the wire form into a 5-inch (12–13 cm) clay pot and plant two well-branched rosemaries on opposite sides of the pot. I have used older, larger plants whose branches extended completely around both lower rings and the crown when first placed in the pot.

The closely wound circles of foliage of a crown ring can be troubled by fungus; follow the preventive measures described above. Rosemary rings especially offer mealybugs a tempting haven. A thorough drenching with an insecticidal soap such as Safer's will eliminate them if detected early. Follow the directions on the container. Alternatively, mealybugs may be removed with cotton swabs soaked with alcohol. Oil sprays are effective in eradicating these pests from some species of plant but are lethal to rosemary and lavender.

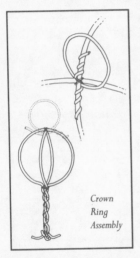

Crown Ring Assembly

Choosing the Right Container

ILLUSTRATIONS FROM MEDIEVAL and early Renaissance manuscripts show topiary trees in tubs and urns decorating European gardens. Standards were raised in square wooden boxes called Versailles tubs topped with corner knobs and raised on feet to promote drainage. Large, heavy clay urns were also widely used for topiaries in ancient times. These had handles so that poles could be inserted for moving them around. Another traditional and still-popular container is made of Italian terra-cotta embellished with ridges and scrolls. These classical styles are compatible with almost all trained plants, especially larger trees such as bay and rosemary.

Styles and types of containers abound—so how does one select the appropriate pot for that special plant? As a rule, a container should be in harmony with the style of the room and its furnishings, and its size should be in correct proportion to that of the mature plant. The plant sculpture is the center of interest, and the container should not be so ornate nor so large that it detracts from the foliage. A sizable tree needs a wooden box, an urn, or a large clay pot. For ease in moving it, a platform on wheels is essential, and this also keeps the pot off the floor for better air circulation.

To determine the size and shape of the container for a topiary, consider the size of the foliage mass, the size of the root ball, and the style that will best harmonize with your decor. Most pleasing to the eye is a pot equal in size to the head of the topiary growing in it. Because the roots of a topiary should be about the same size as its head of foliage, a pot of this size will accommodate healthy root growth. Too large a pot not only looks unbalanced but permits the soil to stay too wet, leading to root rot.

On the other hand, a slow-growing plant with a smaller root ball needs to have its smaller pot placed inside a larger one to balance the top and bottom visually. Stones or gravel in the space between the pots will improve stability. Jardinieres and cachepots should be double-potted with a layer of gravel on the bottom and sand instead of stones on the sides to protect the outer pot.

Top the potting mix with a mulch to slow evaporation in sunny conditions. I like to use green sheet moss (natural, dried moss is available in craft stores) and find that it really cuts down on the need to water on hot summer days. It's easy to remove in cool, damp weather if diseases become a problem. Black or white Japanese river stones are an attractive, but rather expensive, alternative available in better-quality garden catalogs. Because they don't pack tightly together, they permit air to reach the roots.

A good container should not deteriorate from alternate watering and drying out. Where topiaries spend only the summer outdoors, weathering is less of a problem. In climates where winter temperatures do not go below 25°F (-4°C)—the lowest that most of the herbs discussed here can tolerate—clay pots often flake after repeated frosts. This is particularly disappointing when it happens to an expensive Italian terra-cotta or other valuable pot, so locating used pots that have withstood changes in weather is worthwhile.

A Good Container

A good container must hold moisture long enough to supply a plant's needs, yet drain readily: it must have a drainage hole or holes in the bottom.

Finally, a good container should have supports or feet. These enhance drainage and air circulation while discouraging pests such as root mealybugs.

Clay versus Plastic The most common materials used in plant containers are clay and plastic. Each has drawbacks as well as advantages. The porosity that is so desirable in a clay pot, for instance, can be lethal in hot, windy weather outdoors. However, plastic becomes brittle in sunlight even as it prevents rapid evaporation. Its lighter weight can also be a liability in the wind, so it is best to place a plastic pot inside a heavier one of clay or concrete. Because plastic is nonporous, pots made of it need watering less frequently than clay pots. An attractive plastic pot that mimics terracotta in color and texture is now available. It has a rim at the top and a matching saucer, and it comes in a number of sizes.

I believe that the common unglazed clay pot is the "healthiest" for most plants: it allows oxygen to reach the roots and moisture to evaporate through all surfaces. (Glazed clay pots dry more slowly.) They are available in many styles: the ornate Spanish and Italian pots as well as the common "standard" and "azalea" shapes. The standard pot is about as tall as its top is wide; the azalea pot is only three-quarters the height. I rather like the appearance of topiaries in azalea pots, although fast-growing plants such as westringia and myrtle eugenia benefit from the additional volume afforded by the taller standard. All clay pots are measured across the top on the inside.

Clay pots are susceptible to deterioration outdoors, and to green mold and algae and mineral salt deposits, particularly in damp conditions. To some people, a moss-encrusted pot is preferable to a new one in a topiary display, and some even decline to purchase a plant because its pot looks too new. For these tastes, I used to store new pots under greenhouse benches where constant watering ensured a steady inventory of green, slimy pots. Fortunately, algae and moss are not harmful to plants.

Other Alternatives Wooden planters insulate roots from the summer sun. The best materials are redwood or cedar, both of which resist decay as well as hold moisture. These woods need no preservative, but a moisture sealer may be used, if desired. Select wooden planters with tight joints to prevent leakage. However, if you have a leaky one that you'd like to use, you may line it with heavy plastic or a can that has holes punched in the bottom for drainage. Or just use it as a cachepot. In any case, protect the floor!

Metal containers are best reserved for shade-loving plants; in the sun, they can overheat, causing root damage.

Topiary Maintenance

THE ADVICE BELOW applies to all the species described in Plants for Topiaries, page 31. Any exceptions are discussed in that section. Regional differences are discussed on page 30.

Herb topiaries need full sun to look their best. They can be kept outdoors in summer as long as they are thoroughly drenched every day during hot, windy periods. Most plants that I grow are not winter-hardy where I live in Maryland and must be moved indoors to the sunniest spot available before first frost. I rotate the pots one-quarter to one-third turn each week to expose all sides to the sun.

Plants need to be introduced to their new conditions gradually. When moving them outdoors in summer, I place them in a shady spot for two weeks before moving them to full sun. In the fall, I trim the plants lightly and just as gradually move them inside before the first frost.

Soil Topiaries appreciate soil that is light, porous, quick draining, and not too rich. Most herbs thrive in neutral soil, but santolina prefers slightly greater acidity, and lavender, a somewhat alkaline growing medium. Pro-Mix potting mix may be used or a homemade equivalent of three parts potting soil to one part sand or perlite, plus a sprinkle of agricultural lime. Santolina needs no added lime.

I always plant topiaries in clay pots; evaporation through the sides prevents the soil from staying soggy, which can lead to root rot.

Water   If a pot feels light when you pick it up compared to how heavy it feels when wet, *and* if the surface of the soil is dry and the soil ball is beginning to shrink away from the sides of the pot, it's time to water. These judgments take practice but are worth developing. Topiaries grown in containers too large to test by lifting should be checked with a moisture meter (available for about $14). Any reading less than 50 percent calls for watering. Thoroughly drench the plant every time you water but never allow the pot to sit in the drainage water. A soil mixture that drains well (described above) is essential to prevent root rot. At the same time, you must keep the pot from drying out completely. As you become familiar with the plants you are growing, knowing when to water each one will become second nature to you.

If your water is heavily chlorinated (the odor will tell you), let it stand overnight before use. Mineral salts that accumulate in the pot from the use of hard water can burn the roots, but repotting annually in fresh soil and/or flushing monthly with distilled water can prevent this kind of damage.

Fertilizer   For maximum rapid growth, which permits optimal trimming and shaping, I fertilize topiaries—and other herb plants—with a weak liquid fertilizer every two weeks during the active spring and summer growing season. Peters water-soluble fertilizer for foliage plants is good, as is fish emulsion. Reduce the frequency of feeding as growth slows, and don't feed at all if the plant stops growing during winter.

Light   Topiaries growing outdoors need at least five hours of full sun daily to remain compact and bushy. Indoors, a spot with a southern exposure is best. If the natural light is insufficient indoors (plants will begin to look leggy), you may supplement it with two fluorescent tubes: one cool white and one warm white fixed 12 to 16 inches (30–40 cm) above the top of the plants. Herbs need a total of 15 or 16 hours of light per day indoors.

Temperature Daytime temperatures of 60° to 70°F (15–21°C)with a 10 degree drop at night are optimum for herb topiaries, though they can tolerate temperatures 10 degrees lower or higher than these limits without real harm. Many of the plants listed in Plants for Topiaries (page 31) grow well at substantially higher temperatures when planted in the ground, and I have had potted specimens that survived summer greenhouse temperatures of more than 100°F (37°C)with plenty of water to keep them from drying out. Most of the plants do not thrive at lower temperatures, however, and cannot withstand temperatures much below freezing.

Pruning Regular pruning is necessary to maintain the shape of a topiary. During periods of rapid growth in spring and summer, you will probably need to trim it every other week; in winter, rarely or never. Use wide-handled "rabbit ear" shears, curved-blade pruners, or ikebana shears.

Trim the bottom of the plant first; new twigs often turn downward there, especially on westringia and rosemary. After clipping around the bottom of the foliage shape, work up the sides to the top. Cut twigs of large-leaved plants such as bay and eugenia close to a leaf node, but simply trim smaller-leaved plants "haircut" fashion. Branching points don't matter on these, but cut big plants above a "Y" on a branch to stimulate further branching and filling in.

Eventually, a healthy, vigorous, well-maintained topiary *Root* will outgrow its pot, signaling its distress with yellowing *Pruning* leaves, daily wilting, and finally, by ceasing to grow altogether. Radical surgery is in order to revive it. (As these symptoms can signal other problems, check the foliage for pests and the roots for root rot.)

First, cut back the foliage by about one-third; westringia can be pruned much more severely. Then remove the plant from its pot. The roots will be matted around the bottom and sides. At this point, you may decide to move it to a larger pot, in which case slice off about 1/2 inch (1 cm) of the bottom roots and score those left on the sides to promote the formation of new roots. Loosen the central mass of roots and replant in the new pot with fresh soil. Water thoroughly. You may apply a dilute fertilizer, if desired. Keep the plant out of the sun for three weeks, then gradually return it to its usual position. New growth will soon begin to appear.

With more radical pruning, even very mature topiaries—those whose roots have become a dense, knotted mass—can be retained in the same pot indefinitely. To accomplish this, slice off as much as one-third of the root ball and remove up to one-third of the roots from the sides. Cut off any circling roots at the bottom and top. I often cut grooves in the sides of the root mass and pack them with fresh soil. Place new soil in the bottom of the pot, replace the plant, add new soil on the sides, and water it thoroughly. A dose of very weak fertilizer is optional. Move the plant to the shade temporarily after repotting as directed in the previous paragraph.

Herb topiaries can become afflicted with a variety of pests when grown indoors; mealybugs, whitefly, scale insects, and fungus gnats are the most common. I use repeated applications of insecticidal soap, according to the extent of infestation. Plunge the head of a short topiary in a large pail of the solution or thoroughly drench taller ones. Spray or otherwise wet the trunk, too, as mealybugs have a way of hiding out in bark crevices. One treatment may be enough if the problem is detected early; otherwise, you'll need to repeat treatments to eliminate successive generations of the pest as they hatch.

Another effective control for scale and mealybugs is a light dormant oil such as Sun Spray (these are also known as "superior" or "summer" oils), though it is injurious to rosemary and lavender. Do NOT eat trimmings of topiaries that have been sprayed with oil.

Spider mites, which occasionally show up in warm conditions either inside or outdoors, can be discouraged by a strong jet of cold water aimed at the underside of the leaves. The safest pesticides on edible plants for soft-bodied organisms like these mites are insecticidal soaps.

Fungus gnats are small, dark flies that fly up from the soil surface when disturbed; their larvae feed on root hairs, eventually damaging the plant. One home remedy calls for one tablespoon of chlorine bleach in a quart of water used as a soil drench, but it should not be used on young, tender plants. This method is not harmful to larger, established plants.

Diligence in providing the best light, a relative humidity of 50 percent or higher, and good ventilation minimizes pest and disease problems by encouraging healthy plants. Water and/or mist the plants only in the morning and on sunny days. Remove fallen leaves from the pot and prune dead branches with tools sterilized in a flame, as well as picking off dead leaves elsewhere on the plant. If a disease should develop despite these common-sense measures, Safer's garden fungicide is one that may be safely applied to herb plants.

Regional Differences In the North, topiaries spend the summer outdoors, after danger of frost is past, and are returned indoors before the first frost. Keep them in sun but away from strong northeast or northwest winds if possible. Sun may have to be supplemented by fluorescent lights in winter. (All leaves on the top ball of my three-tier eugenia were lost during the winter when the sun didn't reach it. I sawed off the top, leaving two balls that are doing well.)

In the South, plants of Mediterranean origin (most of the herb species grown as topiaries originated there) may be threatened by the occasional cold snaps of late winter when even frost can occur. Container-grown plants should be moved indoors; hardy rosemaries can be left out in the ground if soil is well drained and if the plants are covered as described on page 38. Pests and disease are more of a problem in this region of high humidity, and a site with good air circulation is thus important. Take care not to overwater.

The dry air in the West means few disease problems; at the same time, rapid drying of the soil necessitates frequent watering. Plants can be left outdoors where there is no frost but will need protection indoors in colder areas.

PLANTS
FOR
TOPIARIES

Herbs, like other plants,
grow best when their
cultural needs are met.
Now that you have an
idea of what is involved
in growing herbs as
topiaries, the next step is
to compare the conditions
in your home with the
requirements of some
suitable herbs. The
guidelines contained in
the following descriptions
of the species I've used
should help you decide
which ones are right for
you. All but germander
and dwarf sage, which
winter outdoors in my
herb garden as a
miniature hedge, are
tender perennials.

*Traditional
symbol
of
love,
married
bliss
and
weddings*

Greek Myrtle
(Myrtus communis)

Greek Myrtle
(*Myrtus communis*)

AMONG THE BEST-KNOWN topiary plants is Greek myrtle, a shrubby plant that is easily trained into a variety of forms. Its 1/2-inch (1 cm) glossy, dark green leaves exude a pleasant, peppery scent when clipped. Fuzzy white flowers in spring and summer are followed by shiny black berries.

Greek myrtle was a favorite of the ancients, who used its aromatic leaves for festive occasions such as feasts and weddings. In its native Mediterranean habitat, myrtle is an evergreen bush as tall as 10 feet (3 m), but in most of North America, plants must be moved indoors to a sunny situation in winter. As a topiary, Greek myrtle is usually trained into tight balls which complement its dense foliage.

Those who prefer a less formal design in a standard will undoubtedly appreciate the variegated, or white, myrtle (*M. c.* 'Variegata'), which acquires a graceful, arching form when mature. It is at its best if left to grow naturally after the main stem has been trained to a height of about 14 to 18 inches (35–46 cm) and the branches clipped at the ends. Twigs that grow downward to the soil may be removed, if desired. The white-margined green leaves—others are completely white—contrast beautifully with the nearly black bark, giving an Oriental appearance. Both varieties need full sun, and both produce 1/2-inch (1 cm) pure white flowers with golden stamens, followed by bluish black berries.

Though myrtle topiaries may be summered outdoors, I recommend that they be kept indoors all year to protect them from damaging wind and rainstorms. The general rules for watering and fertilizing are applicable, but because myrtle is highly susceptible to root rot, take special care not to let the soil become soggy.

Myrtle Eugenia
(*Syzygium paniculatum*)

Myrtle Eugenia
(Syzygium paniculatum)

 MYRTLE EUGENIA is a tree that may grow as tall as 40 feet (12 m) in its native Australia; it's grown as a clipped hedge plant in Florida and California. Grown in the ground, its glossy, dark green leaves measure 2 to 3 inches (5–8 cm) long versus 1 to 1 1/2 inches (2.5–4 cm) when container-grown; the new growth emerges pinkish red. The flowers (also larger when grown in the ground) closely resemble those of Greek myrtle (both plants belong to the family Myrtaceae), but the berries of eugenia are larger and fuchsia in color.

A strong grower, eugenia needs transplanting to a larger pot or root pruning at least twice a year. It never seems to get root rot, and radical root pruning does not wilt it. Eugenia topiaries can reach 5 feet (1.5 m) and more unless pruned early to keep them short. They are effective trained into simple shapes of single, double, and triple heads, as well as cones. When trimming eugenia topiaries, I cut right through the leaves; the new growth quickly hides the cuts.

Eugenia, like Greek myrtle, requires indoor winter protection in cold climates but can be moved outdoors in summer if shielded from the wind. It can be raised from cuttings according to the general instructions, but they may require two months or longer to root.

Eugenia is a sun lover; its watering, fertilization, and light requirements are covered in Topiary Maintenance (page 25). Be alert for mealybug and spider mite infestations.

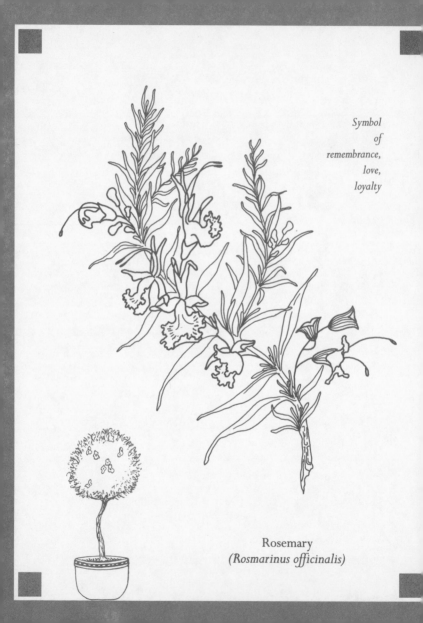

Symbol
of
remembrance,
love,
loyalty

Rosemary
(Rosmarinus officinalis)

Rosemary
(Rosmarinus officinalis)

 WONDERFULLY AROMATIC and flavorful, with a host of culinary uses, rosemary as grown in most of North America is known primarily as a small shrub in pots, though in its native southern Europe, its wood was prized by woodworkers and gathered as firewood. Bancke's *Herbal* of 1525 advises readers to make a box from rosemary wood to sniff to preserve their youth. In his *Paradisus in Sole* (1629), a classic gardening tome, Parkinson refers to lutes and other instruments made from rosemary wood "cloven out into thin boards". He also speaks of women growing rosemary bushes in the shapes of peacocks and cats. Rosemary topiaries are indeed an old custom.

The ancient Romans called the plant *ros marinus*, "dew of the sea," when they encountered it growing on the Mediterranean coast, where it still thrives, misted by frequent fogs. Precisely when rosemary found its way to England is unknown, but its successful adaptation there may be seen in numerous cottage gardens. English colonists introduced the herb to this country in the seventeenth century.

For my rosemary topiaries, I have used the upright cultivars 'Foresteri', 'Joyce DeBaggio' (Golden Rain Rosemary), 'Pine Scented', and 'Benenden Blue', which I train in round-head forms of single, double, and occasionally triple tiers. They may also be grown in conical tree shapes, and spirals are a possibility as well.

Prostrate rosemary cultivars, such as 'Prostratus', may be used to create graceful free-form standards by training the stem upright and allowing the plant to grow naturally at the top, though I have not yet tried this.

A side benefit of rosemary as topiary material is harvesting the trimmings for culinary use when you've let a large plant grow out a little between prunings. Exceptions are the delicately feathery 'Pine Scented' and 'Benenden Blue', which are used strictly as ornamentals.

My rosemary topiaries begin as rooted cuttings which I transfer to progressively larger pots as described in the general instructions (page 13). Rosemary grows fairly rapidly: cuttings made in spring have grown into miniature, 6- to 8-inch-tall (15–20 cm) topiaries by December. Good sanitation (removing dead leaves or any cutting showing signs of disease) while cuttings are rooting will minimize the threat of fungus disease.

I grow my rosemary topiaries indoors, though they will flourish outside in the summer sun if drenched daily in hot weather. Pots of the more tender varieties may be sunk in the garden for the summer and moved back indoors when frost threatens. The upright cultivar 'Arp', which is hardy to 10°F (-23°C), can grow in the ground, but locate it where it will be protected from winter winds. In late fall or when the weather turns cold before frost, wrap the plant, except for the very top, in layers of plastic, such as sheets of thin, flexible packing foam. Secure it with heavy string at 4- to 5-inch (10–12 cm) intervals. A single layer of packing foam can be wrapped around the head of a plant for wind protection in warmer climates.

Indoors or out, rosemary plants need good air circulation to discourage disease organisms. Mealybugs seem to have a special preference for indoor plants and those that have been moved in from outside, so be ever watchful and treat any infestation right away with insecticidal soap.

Rosemary topiaries grow rapidly in spring and summer and will need trimming about every other week to keep their shape. At the same time, vigorous root growth is filling the pot; consequently, you'll probably need to root-prune every spring and fall. Avoid overwatering to prevent root rot. Reasonable care of a carefully sculpted rosemary brings lasting rewards of elegant beauty and usefulness.

Victorian Rosemary
(Westringia rosmariniformis)

Victorian Rosemary
(Westringia rosmariniformis)

 VICTORIAN ROSEMARY is a nonculinary ornamental shrub belonging to the mint family. Native to southeastern Australia and Tasmania, it was popular in Victorian-era conservatories. Both its common and scientific names allude to its supposed resemblance to *Rosmarinus officinalis*, another member of the mint family. Victorian rosemary's 1/2-inch-long (1 cm) silver-green leaves are nearly white underneath, odorless, and shaped like those of Greek myrtle. Its odorless blossoms, borne on the tips of the branches, have pure white square petals, while the branches themselves emerge in whorls around the stem in any number of places, making the plant an excellent subject for training. It grows very vigorously and thus takes shape fairly quickly after training begins. Repotting or root pruning twice annually is necessary.

I have shaped this plant into single, double, and triple balls, and sometimes twisted or braided two or more plants together, which creates a lovely dense head at the top. Take care in manipulating the stems, for they are brittle and can snap under too much pressure. I allow young plants to grow close together in flats without staking or trimming until they are 3 feet (1 m) high or taller, then select several plants of the same height to be potted in a 7-inch (18 cm) pot with a stake. I braid the stems and secure the braid with the same ties that support the plants on the stake. Merely twisting two plants together also makes an attractive standard.

Victorian rosemary is a sun lover, but do not allow a plant, especially one growing in a clay pot, to dry out in hot weather. Be on guard for spider mites at this time and fertilize during the spring-to-fall season of rapid growth as in the general directions.

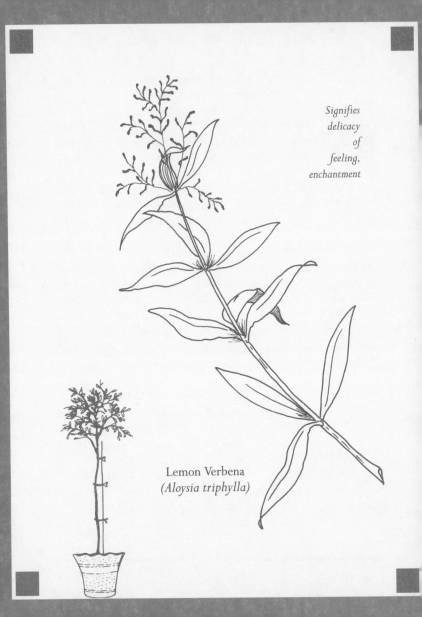

Signifies delicacy of feeling, enchantment

Lemon Verbena
(Aloysia triphylla)

Lemon Verbena
(Aloysia triphylla)

 ONE OF THE FAVORITES of old-fashioned gardens is lemon verbena, brought to Europe from Argentina and Chile by the Spanish in the late eighteenth century. It was cultivated for perfume oil in Spain in early times, but we know little concerning its traditions in the New World.

Lemon verbena is a half-hardy shrub that grows to 10 feet (3 m) or more in its native South America. Its 2-inch-long (5 cm), light green, narrow, prominently veined leaves have a delightful, pungent lemon odor. Pinkish flowers borne at the tips of the branches are insignificant.

The lemon verbena of potpourris, finger bowls, and fruit compotes is also a good subject for standards, as it is a fast grower and makes an attractive, fairly compact head of foliage—not too tight and formal looking. As it is not winter-hardy in our mid-Atlantic area, lemon verbena plants that spend the summer outside require winter protection indoors. Those that are maintained indoors all year tend to keep their leaves in winter, unlike those that have been moved in from outside. Whether outdoors or in, lemon verbena needs full sun and soil that is light, well drained, and alkaline.

Plants do not grow during the winter. If a lemon verbena has been growing outside until cool weather forces it into dormancy, place it in reduced light and keep the soil ball just barely moist. Resume regular watering and return to brighter light in March, and soon new light green leaves will emerge.

Take cuttings in July and August from outdoor plants and in spring from indoor plants. These root readily when the room temperature is at least 65°F (18°C). Monitor plants often for spider mites.

Fringed Lavender
(Lavandula dentata)

*Symbolizes
devotion,
luck,
housewifely
virtue,
acknowledgment*

Fringed Lavender
(*Lavandula dentata*)

 A WONDERFULLY FRAGRANT plant native to Spain and the Balearic Islands, fringed lavender makes a fine topiary whether trimmed close or allowed to grow in a more natural open form. Fragrant, very pale lavender flowers are borne on thin stems emerging from the axils of finely toothed green leaves, though close trimming will prevent blooming.

Standards of fringed lavender are started from cuttings taken with a "heel" (that is, pulled off with a bit of the stem) in spring and early summer. Rooting hormone is not necessary for new shoots. Bottom heat is optional. Cuttings take about six weeks to root. As they are very susceptible to fungus diseases, give them good ventilation and do not mist. Treatment with a fungicide such as Safer's might also be helpful.

Pot fringed lavender in a mixture of three parts potting soil to one part sand, adding 1 teaspoon of agricultural lime to 2 gallons (9 l) of potting mix. It needs a richer soil than English lavender (*L. angustifolia*). Keep it in full sun. Water in the morning preferably, but do not let the pot dry out in warm weather. Good drainage is essential.

A lavender topiary needs frequent trimming during periods of rapid growth to keep its round shape, unless you prefer a more natural appearance and flowers on your plant. A liquid fertilizer applied when you water will help keep it in bloom. The trimmings may be dried for potpourris, sachets, and the like.

Fringed lavender does well outdoors for the summer, but is not winter-hardy in most of North America.

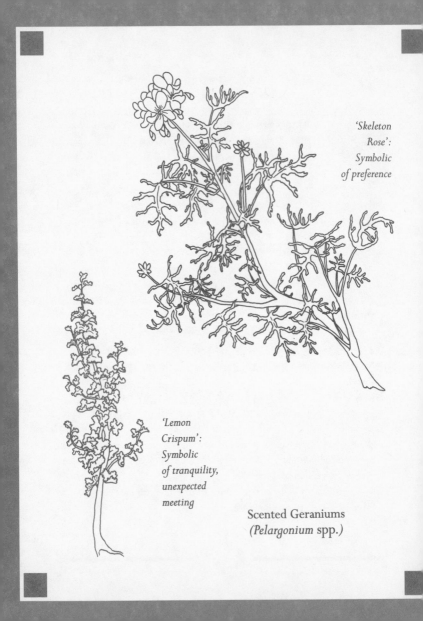

'Skeleton
Rose':
Symbolic
of preference

'Lemon
Crispum':
Symbolic
of tranquility,
unexpected
meeting

Scented Geraniums
(*Pelargonium* spp.)

Scented Geraniums
(*Pelargonium* spp.)

 SCENTED GERANIUMS are native to South Africa. Many varieties were introduced into England early in the seventeenth century, but it was the French who captured the fragrant oil of the rose geranium for the perfume industry more than two centuries later. Many of the scented geraniums can be successfully trained as beautiful, aromatic topiaries, from the tall, large-leaved 'Rose' to the small-leaved kinds such as 'Prince Rupert', which are easily trained as rings. Here are eight types that I've grown as upright standards with single heads:

'Rose' (*P. graveolens*), 'Variegated Rose' (*P. g.* 'Variegatum'), 'Skeleton Rose' (*P. radens* 'Dr. Livingston'), 'Gooseberry' (*P. crispum* 'Variegatum'), 'Lemon Crispum' (*P. c.* 'Minor'), 'Orange' (*P.* x *citrosum*), 'Lime' (*P.* x *nervosum*), and 'Strawberry' (*P.* x *scarboroviae*).

These four work well as rings:

P. crispum 'Prince Rupert', 'French Lace' (*P. c.* 'Prince Rupert Variegatum'), 'Lemon Crispum', and 'Strawberry'.

Scented geraniums are most easily started from cuttings taken in spring and late summer. As mentioned in Starting an Herb Standard (page 12), cuttings are inserted into holes in blocks of Oasis with no rooting hormone. For woodier cuttings taken in winter, a mixture of one part hormone powder, one part powdered fungicide, and ten parts of baby powder will speed the formation of roots yet will not burn soft stems. Bottom heat also will help cuttings root faster. As 'Prince Rupert', 'French Lace', and 'Lemon Crispum' root somewhat less readily and seem to be more susceptible to disease, take a large number of cuttings to ensure enough rooted plants.

Scented geraniums are grown in 4- or 5-inch (10–13 cm) clay pots in light, well-drained potting soil. Training is the same as for other plants; if staked early, most scented geraniums will grow straight stems to heights that vary according to variety. A few of the small-leaved forms can be used for either standards or rings, as may be seen in the lists above. For rings, brittle geranium stems are tied loosely to the wire support instead of being twisted around it like those of rosemary. The foliage soon grows in to cover the ring entirely.

Wedding Rings

One clever idea that I call "wedding rings" involves placing two pots next to each other so that the rings overlap, then planting a small-leaved geranium in each—the growth holds the rings together—and setting the pots inside a large, oval cachepot.

It is important that all surfaces of a geranium plant receive as much sun as possible, as well as good ventilation. Too little and the leaves turn yellow and drop off, which quickly ruins the appearance of a topiary. Regular trimming is necessary during active growth, while very hard pruning in late winter will stimulate bushy new growth as the days lengthen. Both kinds of trimming are especially advisable for a plant that spends its summers outdoors. Potted geraniums dry out easily, but don't make the soil so soggy that oxygen can't reach the roots. If whiteflies become a problem for these plants, use insecticidal soap to get rid of them.

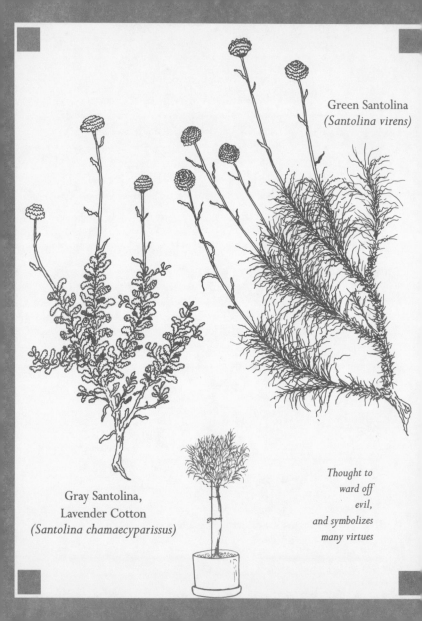

Green Santolina
(Santolina virens)

Gray Santolina,
Lavender Cotton
(Santolina chamaecyparissus)

*Thought to
ward off
evil,
and symbolizes
many virtues*

Green & Gray Santolina
(Santolina virens & S. chamaecyparissus)

 A MEMBER OF THE DAISY FAMILY native to the Mediterranean region, santolina is said to have been one of the first ornamental plants raised in American gardens. Today, this herb is most often planted in sunny borders and knot gardens. If left untrimmed, a profusion of yellow button flowers emerges in early summer.

Santolinas may be shaped into miniature topiaries 10 inches (25 cm) high or less. Standards of the green species, resembling tiny evergreen trees, have become popular for the winter holidays. Santolina's main disadvantage is a strong odor that some people find unpleasant; however, dried clippings can fill sachets to help repel fleas from pet areas. During the Middle Ages, santolina was widely used medicinally.

Santolina can be grown from seed in the South. Elsewhere, plants can be layered to produce more plants: just pile soil over side stems in autumn and when roots form, cut the new plants from the mother plant. Here in Maryland, I start santolina from cuttings taken in spring and early summer. Santolina takes longer to root and grows more slowly than many other topiary herbs—it may take more than a year for a cutting to attain a well-defined form. Clip the tips of new growth to maintain the shape.

Santolinas prefer a well-drained potting medium that is slightly acid; try three parts of potting soil to one part sand or perlite. Santolina topiaries are grown indoors, though they may remain outdoors for the winter in a protected location through Zone 7 if the stem is wrapped with plastic and the plant covered with mulch after the ground is frozen. If spider mites trouble indoor plants, treat them with forceful sprays of cold water or insecticidal soap.

Germander
(Teucrium chamaedrys)

*Signifies
felicity
and
joyousness*

Germander
(Teucrium chamaedrys)

 THIS NATIVE of Europe and southwestern Asia is a small, shrubby, hardy perennial member of the mint family with small, glossy, toothed leaves that are gray beneath. The small, pink, two-lipped flowers are borne on the branch tips. Germander's spreading roots have earned it the specific name *chamaedrys*, "ground oak". A traditional knot garden plant, it was a commonly used medicinal herb in earlier times. This popular hedge and edging plant, still much used in herb and knot gardens, makes a charming miniature standard up to a foot (30 cm) tall.

Cuttings taken in spring and early summer will take a year to become topiaries. After the leader has been pinched off, about six months will elapse while the head develops. Although germander is winter-hardy to Zone 5, I recommend growing germander topiaries indoors as you would santolina. Keep them in full sun and evenly moist. A germander topiary must be staked permanently to prevent the brittle stem from breaking under the weight of the head.

Resin Bush
(Euryops pectinatus)

Resin Bush
(*Euryops pectinatus*)

 THOUGH IT IS not classified as an herb, I have grown topiaries of resin bush along with the herb plants for its profusion of bright yellow daisylike flowers that suggest summer in full bloom throughout winter's gray days and contrast delightfully with the other formal green shapes. The 2-inch (5 cm) blossoms with their large yellow centers—hence the common name "large eyes"—are carried above the ferny silver-gray foliage on thin stems. The deeply lobed leaves can be likened to combs, hence the specific name *pectinatus*.

In its native South Africa, this plant is a vigorous bush, and when trained as a standard, it forms a large, open head 1 1/2 feet (45 cm) or more across that remains in bloom from late fall through spring. The trunk is rather short, about a foot (30 cm) tall, owing to the early three-way branching of the main stem. Two of the three stems may be removed to encourage the remaining one to form a taller standard.

Resin bush will need frequent transplanting to larger pots for the first year. After the plant has reached the desired size, root pruning will be necessary twice annually, but for me, the colorful reward is worth every bit of the work. Give the plant at least half a day of full sun outdoors, as much sun as possible indoors, and keep the soil moist. If you decide to summer it outdoors, soak the pot daily on hot days. Fertilize it during active growth and flowering, alternating between a high-nitrogen formula for foliage plants and one designated for flowering plants. Resin bush should not be fertilized in the North during the winter unless it is blooming—it won't bloom if light levels are too low—but should be fed every month in the South. Be alert for spider mites on this plant.

Dwarf Sage
(Salvia officinalis 'Nana')

Symbolic
of
wisdom,
long life,
esteem,
immortality,
and domestic virtue

Dwarf Sage
(*Salvia officinalis* 'Nana')

THE PUNGENT GARDEN SAGE (*S. officinalis*), native to southern Europe, has long been praised around the world not only for its culinary virtues, but as a promoter of health and longevity; its generic name is from the Latin *salvere*, "to cure." The Romans valued it as a sacred herb, and the Chinese cherished it as a healing plant that also gave long life. We know it today as a rather large, somewhat woody, very hardy shrub whose 3-inch (7–8 cm), pebbly gray-green leaves are an important ingredient of poultry stuffing. Fortunately for those of you who cultivate herbs as topiaries, the dwarf compact cultivar 'Nana' is easily trained as a miniature standard that in early summer rewards the grower with lavender-blue flowers even when the foliage is closely trimmed. Its 1/2- to 1-inch-long (1–2.5 cm) narrow leaves are green with a silvery underside and petiole.

I let a sage plant grow about 10 inches (25 cm) tall before I begin to clip the top foliage. Sage looks best if the foliage is allowed to grow somewhat loose and open. This treatment also provides air circulation and discourages the fungus diseases to which sage is quite susceptible. Other measures to prevent disease include picking off dead leaves, keeping the soil surface clean, and watering only early in the morning. Avoid splashing the leaves when watering.

Topiaries of dwarf green sage can be maintained in 5- or 6-inch (12–15 cm) pots indefinitely with semiannual root pruning. Be alert for aphids, mealybugs, and whiteflies. You may keep sage topiaries either indoors or out. As small pots dry out fast in summer, check them often and keeps the soil remains slightly moist.

Sweet Bay
(Laurus nobilis)

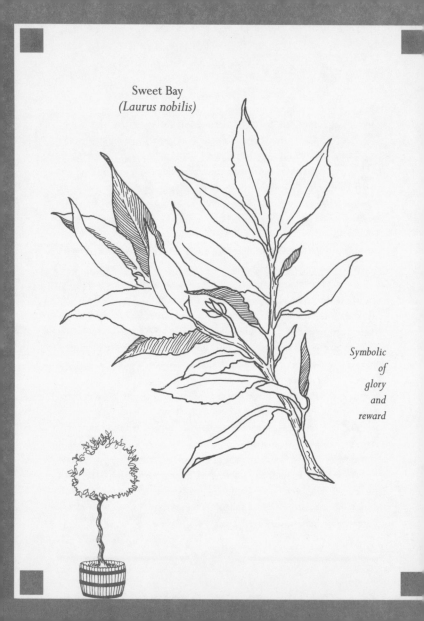

*Symbolic
of
glory
and
reward*

Sweet Bay
(Laurus nobilis)

THE ANCIENT TREE with aromatic leaves that enhance so many foods also makes a stately topiary. Though it can reach a height of 50 feet (15 m) or more in its native Mediterranean habitat, patient nurturing is required for this slow-growing plant which is started from cuttings of new growth taken in late summer. I dip 3- to 4-inch (7–10 cm) cuttings in rooting hormone and insert them singly into 3-inch (7.5 cm) plastic pots of potting mix, then place them in bright indirect light. A layer of tissue paper over them maintains humidity. I remove it after about a week. Bay cuttings may take two months or longer to root.

Newly rooted plants continue growing in the same pots until large enough to be moved to bigger ones—at least a year. Choose a potting medium that is rich, moist, and well drained such as a mixture of humus and sand. Because the leaves are farther apart and trimming is unfeasible, bay plants should be grown a little taller than most topiary starts—6 inches (15 cm)—before training begins. When the stem has reached the desired height, trim the shoots at the top to two or three leaves, which will stimulate the growth of new shoots. When these have filled in, trim them in the same manner until the round shape is formed. Thereafter, maintain with pruning in early and late summer.

As bay tends to branch at the bottom soon after becoming established, pruning for topiaries begins early. When I find older plants with a straight central stem, I trim them as standards after cutting away all side branches. The bay topiaries I've worked with typically measure from 3 to 5 feet (1–1.5 m) tall with fairly open heads of foliage. I save the leaves for the cooking pot or dry them and store them in plastic bags for future use.

Sweet bay is a sun lover, but should be protected from the wind. It must be moved indoors for the winter except in the warmest climates and kept in a sunny location.

Scale insects can afflict bay, in which case a good scrubbing of the leaves and stem with a mild hand soap such as Ivory or castile and a small brush is called for. When a bay plant stops growing and begins dropping its leaves, check to see if it is pot-bound. New leaves may be in evidence, though, even at this time, and they will begin to grow rapidly after root-pruning and repotting.

Bibliography

Bailey, L. H. *The Standard Cyclopedia of Horticulture*. New York: Macmillan Co., 1950.

Bass, Tom, and Barbara Helfman. *Successful Houseplants*. San Francisco, California: Ortho Books, 1984.

Bremness, Lesley. *The Complete Book of Herbs*. London: Dorling Kindersley, 1988.

Clarkson, Rosetta E. *The Golden Age of Herbs and Herbalists*. New York: Dover Publications, 1972.

Clevely, A. M. *Topiary*. London: William Collins Sons, 1988.

Editors of Sunset Books and Sunset Magazine. *How to Grow Houseplants*. Menlo Park, California: Lane, 1974.

Felton, Elise. *Artistically Cultivated Herbs*. Santa Barbara, California: Woodbridge Press, 1990.

Foster, Gertrude B., and Rosemary F. Louden. *Park's Success with Herbs*. Greenwood, South Carolina: Geo. W. Park Seed Co., 1980.

Gallup, Barbara, and Deborah Reich. *The Complete Book of Topiary*. New York: Workman, 1987.

Keville, Kathi. *The Illustrated Herb Encyclopedia*. New York: Mallard Press, 1991.

Kreuter, Marie-Luise. *Natural Herb Gardening*. New York: Macmillan Co., 1983.

Murphy, Wendy B., and the Editors of Time-Life Books. *Gardening Under Lights*. Alexandria, Virginia: Time-Life Books, 1978.

Staff of the L. H. Bailey Hortorium, Cornell University. *Hortus Third*. New York: Macmillan Co., 1976.

Wright, Michael, editor. *The Complete Indoor Gardener*. Green Forest, Arizona: New Leaf Books, 1974.

Zabar, Abbie. *The Potted Herb*. New York: Stewart, Tabori and Chang, 1988.